NEVERSTOP
12 Principles of Success

Cameron Colvin

NEVERSTOP
12 Principles of Success

Cameron Colvin

Circumference Press

Cover art and design:
    Acute Visual Branding & Design - Nonye Ogbodo LTD
    Lolite Media - Mustafa Johnson

Editing and layout by Jonathan Peters, PhD

ISBN: 978-0-9903262-5-0

Printed in the United States of America

CONTENTS

THANK YOU...

Sending gratitude and positive vibes to all the people who have believed in me from the start:

> To my amazing family—You have been my rock

> To the people who are close to me daily—You are my family as well.

There has been good days and bad days, but I remain humbled and focused by the love that you all have given me. You are my motivating force.

Thank you from the bottom of my heart.

Let's stay connected:

www.camcolvin.com
www.neverstopbook.com

Instagram: @drcamcolvin
Twitter: @drcamcolvin
Facebook: @drcamcolvin

Introduction

Neverstop

From an early age, I imagined that I could attain and do everything I wanted. Why? Because I believed that if someone else could accomplish greatness, so could I.

When I was a young boy, I would be in my room practicing my baseball swing, hoping I wouldn't break anything as the bat swished back and forth. I had been watching the famed Ricky Henderson steal base after base on television. And I wanted to attain his greatness.

At other times, I'd watch movies like *Little Giants* or *The Mighty Ducks*, knowing that someday I would be on those grand sports stages. I could literally visualize what it would be like achieve greatness.

One day, I was pretending I was Brett "Hitman" Heart, the famed WWF wrestler. I dove from my bunkbed, crashing to the floor.

When my mother heard the ruckus, she stormed into my room. "Cameron John!"

My sister joined my mother at my bedroom door. "He's crazy, Mom!"

Maybe I was. But I didn't care what my mother and sister thought about my antics. I hoisted my imaginary World Wrestling Title over my head, hearing the crowd cheering in my imagination.

My mother laughed and said, "Have you finished your homework?"

My sister rolled her eyes and went back to her room.

I just smiled, still visualizing my victory. I knew I had a lot to learn about being a sports star, and back then there wasn't much information available. There were only a few websites teaching how things were done in the sports world, and there wasn't enough bandwidth to accommodate videos like we have today.

This meant that if I wanted to learn how to be a sports star, I'd have to watch my idols play on television and then try to replicate what they did. And it was also important that I listened to my coaches. But in the end, I had to make my own path. After all, practice is the father of learning.

My dreams seemed so far away as a child, and I didn't understand the hard work, dedication, and sacrifice it took for the greats to perform at an elite level. But I did know that I couldn't wait to be great. I'd have to start today, learning all that I could and practicing as much as possible.

As I progressed along my journey, I began to realize that nothing would come easily. As I climbed levels of success and merit in life, the amount of work that lay ahead only increased.

Perhaps you have similar grand visions. Maybe you also have the drive it will take to succeed. And maybe you want to learn from those who have achieved greatness in life.

I do not claim to be a superstar, but I've learned from some of the brightest minds there are. My experiences have also given me insights into what it takes to succeed. And I have a desire to give back, and to help others achieve their dreams and reach their full potential.

In my studies of the greats and through my own experiences, I've condensed my learning into 12 principles for success, however you define success. Each one of these principles is necessary for greatness. Skipping even one of them will mean that you will not reach your full potential, and the world will be less without your contribution.

As you partake in reading this book, understand that I can only write from the personal events in my life. I will share the good and the bad I've experienced, and the lessons they taught me. At the end of the day, as we smarten up, we become thankful for all the experiences we've had, both the good and the bad.

Every event in our lives creates a choice, and those choices lead to other choices. These choices stack up to bring us to this very moment in our lives.

Look around. Where are you? What music are you listing to? Were you productive today? Who is next to you? Have you made someone smile today? All of these things came about by your choices.

Follow me through the *12 Principles of Success* system. You are now at a point where you can use these principles to create your own success. What worked for me might not work for you. You'll need to apply these principles to your own life, your current situation, and the goals that you want to achieve in life.

The most important thing, though, is that you get started.

So let's get going!

Neverstop

PRINCIPLE 1

Define Your Vision

The empires of the future are empires of the mind
- Winston Churchill

Vision equals connection. When we set out our visions, we are connecting with something in the universe. This is why the first principle of success is to define your vision. Until you have a vision, you cannot be successful.

Some visions are so clear that it feels like reality, so real that the hair on your arm stands up and you get chills! Some young men envision catching the game-winning pass in the Super Bowl. Or a young lady may see herself sitting at the head of the table of a Fortune 500 company. What is your vision? Is it so real that you can feel it?

The important thing is that you have a vision for your life, and that it is something that truly excites you. Also, make sure you aren't settling. Make your vision for yourself grand. After all, this is your life we are talking about!

Sights from Above

When I was about five years old, I would sit with my father listening to recordings of amazing speeches by Malcom X and Dr. Martin Luther King, Jr. These men were displaying the type of power that would make any father proud to share with his son. My father would say, "Did you hear that! Listen, he's speaking to you! What do you see?"

I had no clue of what my father was getting at when he asked what I could see. All I saw was the dog looking at me through the window, wanting to come inside. Only later would I realize that we was asking me what my vision was when I listened to these great men. He wanted me to do more than simply hear their message; he wanted me to visualize a life where I was applying their great teachings.

When my father passed away a year later, I kept hearing him say, "What do you see?" To this day, his voice rings in my head, "See it!"

Soon after his passing, my mother put me into baseball, and I was absolutely terrible. But my father had instilled in me a desire, and his passing had put a great responsibility on me. So it didn't matter that I was terrible at baseball, I knew that I had to work hard to be great. I would stay late after practice, working with my coach. Soon, I was receiving Allstar nominations, batting lead-off, and even playing in the outfield like my idol, Ricky Henderson.

Thanks to my father, I saw my vision, and did everything in my power to achieve it.

Growth of Vision

By the time I was 15, I was developing into a notable wide receiver at De La Salle High School in Concord, California. I was a good football player when I was young, and thankfully the Universe provided me with a high school program that focused on *Les Hommes De Foi*, "men of faith." The program was legendary, so much so that a movie about the program called *When the Game Stands Tall* was produced. It covers my senior year and the year following my graduation.

Playing for a program such as De La Salle raised the stakes for me. As a kid, I had envisioned playing on this scale! But I had no clue when and how this vision would come true. But playing for De La Salle was the ultimate demonstration of my manifestation skills.

I'm proud to be part of De La Salle's winning streak. There has never been a coach like Bob Ladouceur. Coach's success with us was based on his dedication to each of us as well as his understanding of the game. He did so much more than train us to be superior athletes, he wanted us to be upstanding men. And his program reflected this dedication.

For instance, every Thursday before a Friday night game, our team would attend a "chapel." Each position group would take on the responsibility of leading the session. There would be quotes and readings from John Wooden, Buddha, Tony Robbins, and more. Then, as the team focused on those powerful words, we would lay in complete silence to manifest and visualize the success we'd have the next evening.

Like a movie playing in my mind, I saw myself lining up against my opponent. I would calculate every move during the game. Then, I'd celebrate the success I'd have when we won the game. It became an out-of-body experience for me. I'd see the game play out, my teammates carrying out their assignments, and our massive success being celebrated after the game clock reached zero.

As we "awoke" from our session, it was like a new found confidence had been instilled in us. Guys smiled, hugged, and expressed the ultimate gratitude towards one another. We were all connected by our vision. We knew that we had already won the game.

I was only 15 years old when I began learning these lessons from Coach Ladouceur. He taught each of us the lessons of commitment and reliability. We were given the opportunity to write goals, envision them, and commit to getting them done. But most important, we were committed to our teammates. I could not succeed without them, and they were relying on me to do my part so that each of us would achieve our vision of victory.

Our commitments were based on our visions. We set lofty goals and visualized what we needed to do to get to where we wanted to go. I'm not saying the process was easy. But when you set a goal, and someone is helping you attain it, it puts the pressure on you to get it done. The last thing I wanted to do was let down my teammates.

You can do the same. Visualize your goals. Stretch yourself when you think of victories you want in life. Then, as you visualize, see yourself facing obstacles and overcoming them. Notice what it feels like to get closer and closer to your goal. Then, finally, feel the celebration of achieving your goals. You can do this for short-term and long-term goals.

It is also important to share your vision with someone. Find someone who has a similar passion as you, and work with them to get things done. Because once you have a "team" helping you achieve success, you'll be accountable to them and they will be accountable to you. Together, you can work toward becoming what you were meant to be.

Example of a Famous Visionary

Oprah Winfrey

What chances of success would you give a poor woman born in the backwoods of Mississippi to a single, teenage mother, later raised in inner-city Milwaukee, raped at nine years old, then, at 14, gave birth to a son who died shortly thereafter?

Grim chances. Unless that woman happens to be Oprah Winfrey.

Oprah landed her first radio job in high school. She soon transferred to daytime talk TV. After successfully powering up ratings for a Chicago TV show, she started her own production company. That production company, Harpo, launched an empire. *The Oprah Winfrey Show* is the highest-rated talk show in TV history, and has won several Emmy Awards

Oprah is an amazing philanthropist who donates a cut of her $1.3 billion net worth to a variety of causes benefiting women, children, and families.

PRINCIPLE 2

Do What is Necessary (Even When You Don't Want To)

Don't believe what your eyes are telling you. All they show is limitation. Look with your understanding, find out what you already know, and you'll see the way to fly.

- Richard Bach

What's the point of doing something if you don't like doing it? Because it might bring you closer to your vision and goals. But make sure it *is* bringing you closure to what you want in life. If it isn't, don't do it!

Plenty of people get up in the morning and go through a rut. They have nothing to look forward to in their day. They don't have a passion for what they are doing, and what they are doing isn't taking them anywhere.

Not us! Everyday is an adventure. We live every day to the fullest, and we aim to get the most out of our 24 hours as possible. Everything we do is taking us closer to where we want to be.

Don't get me wrong, we will have to do things we don't like doing, but our attitude will change once we realize that what we don't like doing will give us what we want.

For instance, my least favorite subject in school was biology, and yes, I had to go to class. I didn't like the class, and dreaded going. The quizzes and tests were miserable. But I knew that to be the type of athlete I wanted to be, I needed to do well in school. So I studied and did my best in biology. I knew that it was something I had to triumph over, no matter how much I didn't like it.

I can tell you, now I am *absolutely intrigued* with the study of living organisms: plants, bacteria, even bugs! Most important for athletes is the study of physiology. The human body is a pure work of art to me! And I love to study it. If you want to run faster or jump higher, you can do so by understanding what fuels your body, what foods help you think and feel better! You can also study how the body moves so you can improve your form. You can train in a manner that is scientifically proven to improve your game.

So something I didn't like in high school is now important to me, even interesting.

You Won't Know Unless You Try

Sometimes we assume we won't like something even when we haven't tried it. But we never really know what we like unless we try it. One of most important things that I have learned along my journey is that the person who does not attempt to move outside of their comfort zone limits themselves from the start. There are so many opportunities and possibilities out there, that if we limit ourselves to what we like and think we'll like, we will miss out. But if we at least try something, we will find that we do, in fact, enjoy it, or that the activity will lead to other opportunities. The important thing is that you give it your all.

You can only be passionate about activities you've already tried. But when you're young, you probably haven't tried much of the world; therefore, you don't really know what you might enjoy. Worse, if you only do what you like right now, you will limit your possibilities.

For instance, many young people are passionate about sports and music, but these are hard to turn into good jobs. Yes, there are some musicians and athletes who make a good living and live amazing lives, but there are only so many of them. And there is only so much you can achieve in life. Musicians are limited by the likes and dislikes of their audience, and athletes eventually get too old to play. If you only focus on what you're passionate about right now, you will only consider things that are immediately satisfying. You won't ask bigger questions like, "What can I do that's valuable to the world?"

So when you're young, try as many things as possible. Expand your horizons. Discover what you can do that will be meaningful and help others.

Try this exercise when you are being limited by what you don't like:

Don't Like Exercise

Make a list of ten things you are willing to try that you think you will not like. Maybe it's something like getting up an hour earlier, eating a healthy vegetable, doing chores, anything!

1.

2.

3.

4.

5.

6.

7.

8.

9.

10.

Now, for the next ten days, try one of these things at least once. See how the quality of your life changes when you do the things you "think" you won't like.

Be Who You Are

Peer pressure makes us do crazy things! A great key to success is to be exactly who you are. The beautiful thing about life is we get to wake up and be exactly who we want to be. There is only one of us, and we are all unique in some way.

Lots of people get tangled in feeling that they have to be someone else in order to be accepted. But your gut instincts and self awareness will tell you if you are on the right path for you! Remember that as we grow mentally and physically, our life interests will shift with us, and that is OK!

"Dream chasing," as we call it, will take us many places. It will open our minds and spirits to become our "higher self." In the end, there is nothing more satisfying than being the best self you can be.

Follow Your Passion

The idea of following your passion does not mean there is only one path for you. I thought I would be a pro football player forever! But that did not happen. And I haven't been disappointed by where life has taken me, because I can continue to follow my passion.

The best thing we can do is focus on taking good steps in the right direction everyday. When we do this, we will continually improve.

And we need to have the right people on our "team." Remember, teamwork makes the dream work! Any successful person will tell you they did not reach the levels of success by themselves. If you are starting a business, putting together a band, or playing an organized sport, it is very important that you build a solid team and be the best team member you can possibly be.

Make sure that each team member is working toward your vision and that everyone is passionate about success. But also make sure that as you change, your team changes with you. Stay focused on your vision and passion, and you will be successful!

Do What Is Necessary

When I talk about pursuing a vision and having passion, too often people just focus on what feels good, what they want to do. But success does not come easily, and there will be many times when you'll be called upon to do things you don't like doing.

It's important that you don't avoid doing the unpleasant things, because often these are the very things that need to be done to reach your potential.

The test of a person is how well they persevere under pressure. And the best way to practice this perseverance is to do things we don't like doing.

So make sure you do what needs to be done, even if it's not something you like, and you will be amazed at the opportunities that come your way!

Examples of People Who Followed Their Passions

Bill Gates
Long before he created Microsoft, Bill Gates was an amateur programmer. He was so passionate about computers that in the eighth grade, he managed to get excused from math class to design things like early video games.

Walt Disney
What did Disney spend his time doing while growing up? Drawing! He was pretty young when he sold his first drawing (of a neighbor's horse). Disney launched several unsuccessful animation companies before coming up with Mickey Mouse in 1928.

Kevin Plank
As a football player at the University of Maryland, Plank designed shirts that could wick away sweat. He convinced his former teammates to wear them. Many of these guys went on to play professionally and shared the shirts with their teammates. The company that resulted, Under Armour, had $2.3 billion in revenue in 2013.

Debbi Fields
Debbi Fields was only 20 years old when she started selling homemade chocolate cookies—a tiny business that she and her husband, Rands Fields, ultimately grew into Mrs. Fields. The company now has 390 locations around the United States and 4,000 employees.

PRINCIPLE 3

Surround Yourself with Good People and Build a Team

> *Individual commitment to a group effort—that is what makes a team work, a company work, a society work, a civilization work.*
>
> -Vince Lombardi

Synergy in team building is an art. To have like-minded people share passion, vision, and work ethic is absolutely key. My successes have come from mastering skills, visualizing victories, and putting the right people together to get the job done!

During my days prior to going to the University of Oregon, I had a scholarship offer from every school in the country except three, and those were Ivy League institutions who only accepted guys with a 4.0 GPA.

As an athlete, I would spend days analyzing current rosters and scouting reports to see what guys were going where. It was very important to me to be around guys who shared the same visions and hunger for the game as I did. I wanted a good team that would help me reach my vision.

Miami, USC, Michigan, Florida State, and Oregon were my top five choices. I was ranked between number one and number three in the country for my position, and I had a five-star ranking, along with numerous awards, so I had plenty of options. Also, De la Salle High School had won 151 consecutive games, and my class had achieved three national titles playing some of the best schools in the nation. So not only had I excelled as an athlete, but I was also supported by an amazing team.

During the recruiting period, my teammates and I communicated more than ever before. We called one another constantly to see what schools were interested in us and what each other's thoughts were about those schools. This was before the instant access of social media.

As the recruiting went on, three of my De La Salle teammates also received offers from the University of Oregon. And three older guys from our school were already there. In the end, there would be eight De La Salle graduates on the Oregon Ducks' roster, including TJ Ward who went on to the Denver Broncos. It was unheard of to have this many guys from one high school on one college team. But each of us knew the training that the other men had received. We knew we could count on each other as we worked to achieve our goals.

Unfortunately, we did lose our brother Terrance "TK" Kelly to a senseless act of violence a day before we would leave for college. It was a great loss that was felt by every team member both personally and as a team.

As you are building your team or becoming a part of a team, here are a few skills that you should personally focus on to create the best team and to become the best team member possible!

Commitment:

- Do team members want to participate on the team?
- Do team members feel the team mission is important?

- Are members committed to accomplishing the team mission and expected outcomes?

- Do team members perceive their service as valuable to the organization and to their own careers?

- Do team members anticipate recognition for their contributions?

- Do team members expect their skills to grow and develop?

- Are team members excited and challenged by the team opportunity?

Creative innovation:

- Is the organization really interested in change?

- Does it value creative thinking, unique solutions, and new ideas?

- Does it reward people who take reasonable risks to make improvements?

- Does it provide the training, education, access to books and films, and field trips necessary to stimulate new thinking?

Problem solving:

You may have heard the quote, "A problem clearly stated is a problem half solved." Although it seems trivial, the team should not take clearly stating the problem lightly. It is important to begin the problem-solving journey with a clear, concise problem statement. If this is not done properly, it could lead to excessive time spent on identifying issues and the team may be predisposed to a particular solution.

Communication:

- Are team members clear about the priority of their tasks?
- Is there an established method for the team to give feedback and receive honest performance feedback?
- Does the team understand the complete context for their existence?
- Do team members communicate clearly and honestly with each other?
- Do team members bring diverse opinions to the table?
- Are conflicts addressed?

Collaboration:

- Does the team understand team and group processes?
- Do members understand the stages of group development?
- Are team members working together effectively?
- Do all team members understand the roles and responsibilities of team members, team leaders, team recorders, and so on?

Build your team; lead your team! These base skills can be implemented in any environment. Continue to focus on growing yourself before you help others. The beauty of having team members is that you can help each other improve, grow, and reach goals.

PRINCIPLE 4

Communicate

Take advantage of every opportunity to practice your communication skills so that when important occasions arise, you will have the gift, the style, the sharpness, the clarity, and the emotions to affect other people.

- Jim Rohn

Think about the times when things didn't go well between you and someone else, when communication broke down between you. Could you have simply communicated something to them and made the situation much better? How much time and effort could you have saved? How much further along would you be?

The greatest success stories in the world have come from some of the greatest communicators. That is why I have dedicated this entire chapter to communication.

Communicate or Sink

Let me tell you about a time when my communication skills were put to test.

One early morning, I entered my mother's bedroom to let her know I was ready to go school. I found her just sitting there.

I asked, "Are you OK?"

"I'm fine," she smiled. "Go ahead to school. I'll see you later."

My mother had been battling minor health issues for a few years, but nothing serious. So while it was odd to see her just sitting in her room, I wasn't too worried.

Around noon, my sister called me to tell me Mother had gone to the hospital to "get checked out."

As soon as I could, I called my mother. She sounded fine while she told me they were going to run tests on her. She was going to stay over night in the hospital, but she'd see me tomorrow.

The next day, though, we received a call from the hospital stating that she had slipped into an unresponsive coma.

I was shocked. How had things taken such a turn so quickly? She seemed fine the day before. Now she was lying in a bed unable to even smile at me.

My mother was such a strong and resilient woman that I honestly felt that she was going to pull through and recover.

But when another week had passed, and my mother wasn't showing signs of coming out of her coma, my sister and I knew we had some extensive choices to make. There came a time when we knew we needed to say our final goodbyes to an amazing woman who had been a true rock to not just us, but to an entire community. My sister and I came to the conclusion that we would have to pull the plug on my mother and see if she could sustain life without all the machines.

The next day, I was in class when they unhooked my mother from the life-support system. I had not told anyone what was going on in my personal life, so I sat alone in my thoughts, missing the woman who had been such a force in my life, who had comforted me when my father died and continued to guide me throughout childhood. I loved her so much.

It wasn't until after football practice that night that I found out that she had passed away. My sister told me that Mother held on for a few hours, but then slipped away.

It seemed as if life had come to a halt. My rock, my protector, was no longer able to show me the way. My mother had prepared me for this moment by telling me she would not be around forever, and I would have to step up one day. But I wasn't ready to let her go.

At the young age of 15, the thought of not having any parents was rather frightening. I was entering into a scenario that I had never anticipated. Who was going to give me advice? Who was going to pick me up when I was down? Who was going to love me unconditionally? Where was I going to go? My mind took on hundreds of thoughts in an instant.

My team gathered around me when they heard the news. As I cried, my mother's favorite saying rang in my mind, "You will never be given anything you cannot handle." Even though her death seemed like more than I could handle, I was surrounded by my brothers. They would support me. Their love motivated me to stay the course.

My communication skills had to quickly go to work. Funeral arrangements had to be made. There were also living arrangements, car rides, bills, lawyers, family members to inform—a lot of things that a 15-year-old

doesn't normally deal with. I had to man-up and step up.

My sister and I worked as a team, communicating our next steps in life. Our mother and father had given us the belief that no matter how hard things may be, you must stick to the foundational skills and press through.

What is effective communication? It's about more than just exchanging information. It's about understanding the emotions and intentions behind the information people share. You want to make sure your message is received and understood by someone in exactly the way you intended.

Effective communication is also a two-way street. It's not only how you convey a message, but also how you listen. You want to gain the full meaning of what's being said, and make the other person feels heard and understood.

More than just the words you use, effective communication combines a set of skills including nonverbal communication, engaged listening, managing stress in the moment, the ability to communicate assertively, and the capacity to recognize and understand your own emotions and those of the person you're communicating with.

Communication comes in two forms: Internal (the things we picture and feel), and external (the words, tonalities, facial expressions, postures and physical action). External communication will determine your level of success with others. It's not about how you feel; it is about how you gauge your interpretation of things.

Successful communication comes when we control our internal communication and make sure external communication successfully communicates our pictures and feelings. If the two are out of sync, we will confuse the person we're communicating with. But when we master our external communication, we will be successful.

Communication is power!

A Short List of Great Communicators

Jay-Z: Born Shawn Corey Carter in 1969, Jay-Z is the most financially and culturally successful hip-hop artist, rapper, songwriter, producer, and entrepreneur in the world. According to *Forbes*, his net worth is about $450 million, and he's sold more than 50 million albums worldwide. He also has 14 Grammies under his belt, and there are surely more to come.

He communicates through the fashion world with his successful Rocawear line that caters to both adults and children. A film company, upscale sports bars, and part ownership of the New Jersey Nets round out his impressive portfolio. As he rapped, "I'm not a businessman/I'm a business, man," this man sparked the international hip-hop movement. He is a communications agent for change as well being on his way to the Billionaire's Club.
Take-away: See beyond trends to the bigger picture, and capitalize on it.

Tony Robbins: The intelligentsia might criticize this self-help master—but who cares? Robbins's gifts as a motivational speaker, bestselling author, "firewalker," and success coach are unparalleled in the personal development business.

Starting out with little in the way of education or financial resources, he began by promoting Jim Rohn's seminars before embarking on his own work as a self-help coach. Now, Robbins is an international phenomenon with success that his colleagues dream about achieving. More than four million people from around the globe have participated in his programs, lectures, workshops, and one-on-one sessions including George H. W. Bush, Bill Clinton, Mikhail Gorbachev, Anthony Hopkins, Pamela Anderson, and Quincy Jones.

Robbins walks his talk, and he has proven that his dynamic philosophy works. Who knows how many great communicators he has spawned.

Take-away: Believe what you say and others will too.

Richard Branson: The mogul might be best known for his Virgin Group of more than 400 companies, including an ultra hip airline—and that's saying a lot since most airlines suffer from dismal customer service and dreary accommodations. He's also a consummate adventurer and world traveler, whose attempts to break world records and pull off PR stunts have captured the imagination of admirers the world over.

Branson invests his time and money in many causes, from encouraging entrepreneurship (he still considers himself one), to improving economic conditions in Africa, to saving the lemur in Madagascar and the polar bear in Canada. In the process, he's been able to bring attention—and funds—to causes that might be lost without his efforts. While he has claimed that he has to force himself to deliver speeches, when he does, you can hear a pin drop. No one wants to miss a word this mega-brander has to say.

Take-away: If you want to grow, don't just work on your business; work on the business of your business.

Jack Welch: He has been called the greatest CEO in America. In practical terms, he earned the name because of General Electric's unparalleled record of growth over more than two decades while he was chairman and CEO (1981-2001). He has attributed his success to an ability to focus on solutions and execute them using the right people.

In order to do what Jack has done, you have to know how to communicate a message. His secret? "In leadership, you have to exaggerate every statement you make. You've got to repeat it a thousand times... Overstatements are needed to move a large organization."

Of course, you have to back up words with action, otherwise what you say will never be taken seriously. Today, when Welch gives a speech, he embodies true American optimism and risk-taking.

Take-away: Words are most valuable when backed up by deeds.

Neverstop

PRINCIPLE 5

Give More Than You Expect to Receive

Effective philanthropy requires a lot of time and creativity—the same kind of focus and skills that building a business requires.

—Bill Gates

Give from the heart! I have always felt that when doing something for another person, it should be out of the goodness of your heart. You want to give without expecting to get something in return. That's giving from your heart.

People often think of giving money when they think of giving. But that is only a small part of giving. Check out these things you could do that don't involve money:

1. Help teach a child to read

2. Help cook and/or serve a meal at a homeless shelter

3. Gather clothing from your neighbors and donate it to a local shelter

4. Make "I Care" kits with combs, toothbrushes, shampoo, etc. for the homeless

5. Pack and hand out food at a local food bank

6. Adopt a "grand friend" and write them letters and visit them

7. Rake leaves, shovel snow, clean gutters, or wash windows for a senior citizen

8. Pick up groceries or medicine for an elderly person

9. Go for a walk with a senior citizen in your community

10. Deliver meals to homebound individuals

11. Hold an afternoon dance for your local nursing home

12. Teach a senior friend how to use a computer and the Internet

13. Paint a mural over graffiti

14. Tutor a student who needs help learning English or another subject

For the past few years, my company, Rise Above Enterprises, has connected with a number of nonprofit organizations, and we have made some great contributions in a number of communities.

I remember when we kicked off our third annual Rise Above Turkey Give Away at The East County Boys and Girls Club in my hometown of Pittsburgh, CA.

The event has grown tremendously, and we have had support from amazing companies like Chevys, Google,

Kenion Training, and Maria Jones Law Firm. We support local families by giving them holiday meals. So far, we have given out 600 turkeys and meals. It's amazing to see the looks of appreciation on those families faces!

My second favorite giving event is when we join forces with Linking Sports and Communities of Phoenix, Arizona. Together, we put on AZ Sports Youth Day. This is a day where we volunteer to give the youth in Chandler, Arizona a day of motivation and encouragement by using sports and education. Hosting on-field football activities for hundreds of youth is fun.

I also have had the opportunity to speak on a panel with such people as fellow former NFL football player Andre Thurmond. I tell my story of adversity and development, and ask the younger generation, "What do you want to be when you grow up?"

Some reply, "I'm not sure."

Others say things like, "A doctor," "A fireman."

I then tell them, "If you think it, you can achieve it."

I want them to achieve their full potential. I don't want them limited by faulty thinking or laziness. I've been given so many amazing opportunities, and some

of the greatest people in the world have helped me succeed. Now it is my turn to inspire other young people.

For you, it all starts with making good choices and
contributing to society. If you are interested in donating
your time and efforts, do it! The feeling you will have
will be truly amazing.

You'll be surprised by the rewards you will receive
when you give without expectations of a return.

A Short List of People Who Do or Did Great Things for Their Communities:

Mark Zuckerburg

Priscilla Chan

Maya Angelou

David Sainsbury

Warren Buffet

Bill Gates

Melinda Gates

Ann Gloag

Craig Silverstein

Natalie Orfale

Craig Silverstein

Princess Diana

Mother Teresa

Mariah Carey

Richard Branson

PRINCIPLE 6

Use Mistakes as an Improvement Tool

A man must be big enough to admit his mistakes, smart enough to profit from them, and strong enough to correct them.

- John C. Maxwell

Unfortunately, we will make mistakes in life. But the beautiful thing is very few mistakes will actually kill us. Better yet, we have the opportunity to learn from those mistakes, and to make sure we never repeat them.

But most people will either make a mistake and not learn from it, or they will become too afraid to attempt anything that they can fail at. Both situations lead to failure. If we don't learn from our mistakes, we'll make them again. On the other hand, if we never make mistakes, we are probably not growing and improving.

When I was playing for the Oregon Ducks, my wide receiver coach gave me a simple rule, "You have to have tough skin and not become a repeat offender." He meant that if you want to achieve your goals, you have to be willing to take criticism and learn from it.

Most importantly, you have to avoid making the same mistakes twice. If you become a person who simply does not learn from the first mistake, you will

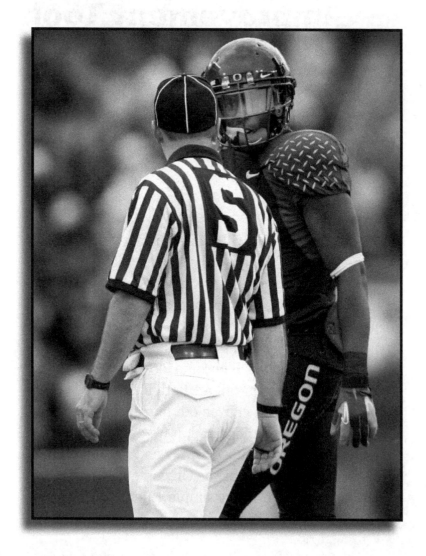

be looked at as unreliable, untrustworthy, and someone people will surely avoid.

Success and Failure Leave Clues

As we go through life, we begin to identify that there
is a pattern for success. But did you know there is also
a pattern for failure? Just as successful people have
habits, so do unsuccessful people. At times, knowing
what *not* to do will help you know what to do.

Unsuccessful people continue to fail because they
see problems in every opportunity. They find fault with
everything. For instance, they complain that the sun
is too hot. They curse the rain for ruining their plans.
They blame the wind for messing up their hair. They
think that everyone is against them. They see problems, but never the solutions.

For these people, every little bit of difficulty is ex-
aggerated to the point of tragedy. They regard failures
as catastrophes. They become discouraged easily instead of learning from their mistakes. They never seem
to move forward because they're afraid to come out of
their comfort zones.

Unsuccessful People Act Before They Think

Unsuccessful people move based on impulse. They
desire immediate gratification. If they see something
they like, they buy it without any second thoughts. Then
they see something better and regret their original pur-
chase. Or maybe they get into impulsive relationships
that end in disaster. They make decisions on the spot

and don't think about the future or the consequences of their actions and decisions.

Unsuccessful People Talk More Than Listen

Unsuccessful people want to be the star of the show. They say things that make them seem important, even to the point of lying. Most of the time, they are not aware that what they're saying makes no sense. When other people advise them, they close their ears because they would rather die than admit their mistakes. In their mind, they're always right. They reject suggestions or help from others because it makes them feel inferior.

Unsuccessful People Quit Quickly

Successful people treat failures as steppingstones to success. Those who seldom succeed usually call it quits at the first signs of failure. At first, they are excited to start a new endeavor, but then they lose interest quickly, especially when they encounter obstacles. Then they search for a new goal, business, career, or relationship. But with all of these new efforts, they get the same results. People who consistently fail don't have the persistence to work though their problems and obstacles to fulfill their dreams.

Unsuccessful People Try to Bring Others Down to Their Level

Misery loves company, and unsuccessful people envy other people who are successful. Instead of working hard to be like successful people, they spread rumors and try every dirty trick in the book to bring successful people down. They could have asked these successful people for help, but they're too proud. They would rather make successful people unsuccessful than learn from them.

Unsuccessful People Waste Their Time and Yours

Unsuccessful people don't know what to do. They often eat too much, drink too much, watch TV and sports for hours, or play video games all day. They have no thoughts whatsoever about what direction their life is going. Most of their time is spent on instant gratification, and they avoid thinking about the quality of their life.

Unsuccessful People Take the Easy Way Out

Imagine there are two roads to choose from. Unsuccessful people will choose the wider road with less reward than the narrower road with much greater reward. They avoid anything that may cause temporary hardship. They want an easy life.

What unsuccessful people don't understand is that you get out what you put in! Effort and action will not go unnoticed. If unsuccessful people would be willing to sacrifice a little, they would gain a lot more.

Successful individuals reach their goals, dreams, and desires through trial and error. They never give up. They do what it takes to create what they desire. Success is not difficult. All it takes to succeed is to discover what unsuccessful people do—then do the opposite!

Choices Lead to Other Choices

In life, we will always have choices. Our lives are filled with them. There are simple choices like what to wear, how to respond to someone, or even what to eat. All these things potentially lead to a bigger picture.

In its simplest sense, decision-making is the act of choosing between two or more courses of action. In the wider process of problem-solving, decision-making involves choosing between possible solutions to a problem. Once we choose, we will be offered more choices. In this way, our path in life lays out in front of us.

Intuition

Decisions can be made through either an intuitive or reasoned process, or a combination of the two. Intuition is using your 'gut feeling' about possible courses of action.

People talk about intuition as if it was a magical 'sense.' Intuition is actually a combination of past experience and your personal values. It is worth taking your intuition into account because it reflects your learning about life. Examine your gut feeling closely, especially if you have a very strong feeling against a particular course of action.

One important thing to remember about correcting mistakes and making great choices is that our gut and intuition will tell us what we need. Life is a feeling process. Listen to your soul!

Reasoning

Reasoning is using the facts and figures in front of you to make decisions. It has its roots in the here-and-now. While reasoning has its place, it can ignore emotional aspects of the decision, and in particular, issues from the past that may affect the way the decision is implemented.

On the other hand, intuition is a perfectly acceptable means of making a decision, although it is generally more appropriate when the decision is simple in nature or needs to be made quickly. Otherwise, it is good to support our intuition with reasoning.

People often say they find it hard to make decisions. Maybe they put off making decisions by endlessly searching for more information or getting other people to offer recommendations. While they gather information, opportunities pass them by. When they don't make a decision, they are in fact deciding not to take an action.

What Can Prevent Effective Decision-Making?

There are a number of problems that can prevent effective decision-making. These include:

1. **Not Enough Information**: If you do not have enough information, it can feel like you are making a decision without any basis. Take some time to gather the necessary data to inform your decision, even if the timescale is very tight. If necessary, prioritize your information gathering by identifying which information will be most important to you.

2. **Too Much Information**: When we have too much conflicting information, it is impossible to see "the forest for the trees." You don't want so much information that you aren't able to make the decision.

3. **Too Many People**: Making decisions by committee is difficult. Everyone has their own views and their own values. And while it's important to know what these views are, and why and how they are important, it may be essential for one person to take responsibility for making a decision. Sometimes, any decision is better than no decision.

4. **Vested Interests**: Decision-making processes often flounder under the weight of vested interests. These vested interests are often not overtly expressed, but they may become a crucial blockage. Because they are not overtly expressed, it is hard to identify them clearly, and therefore address them. But it can sometimes be possible to explore vested interests with someone outside the process. It can also help to explore the rational/intuitive aspects with all stakeholders, usually with an external facilitator to support the process.

5. **Emotional Attachments**: People are often attached to the status quo. Decisions tend to involve the prospect of change, which many

people find difficult. Remember that "deciding not to decide" is also a decision.

In life, we need to make decisions, even if those decisions end up being wrong or create unintended consequences. As long as we are able to learn from our mistakes, the long-term results of a bad decision can actually work out for the best. We just have to have confidence that we will learn from our mistakes and be dedicated to being a better person.

PRINCIPLE 7

Be Prepared

There are no secrets to success. It is the result of preparation, hard work, and learning from failure.

—Colin Powell

It's been said, "Success favors the prepared." Take notice of how some of the greatest achievers in history have prepared long before they achieved success. Payton Manning, Joe Montana, Martin Luther King Jr are prime examples.

The famous Nebraska football coach Tom Osborne once said, "I celebrate a victory when I start walking off the field. By the time I get to the locker room, I'm done." He was saying that once he was in the locker room, he was preparing for the next game.

Each Level Demands More

My coaches were always preparing. Starting in high school at De La Salle with Coach Bob Ladouceur, then college ball with Mike Belotti and Chip Kelly, and in the pros as a 49er with the Super Bowl winning coach Mike Martz, the one common trait these coaches all had was running an efficient meeting and tough practices. They focused on preparing us for our opponents. It was up to us, as players, to study and master the playbook. After all, the mental aspect is 90% of performing at a high level.

There is nothing worse than not being prepared to complete a task. For example, most top students simply don't magically ace midterms. They study! They find a formula to take all the compiled information and break it down so it makes sense for them and so they can remember it. Once test day arrives, they are prepared to succeed.

We all know the guy who got in front of the class for a presentation, and he has no clue about what he was going to say. Remember to prepare and not embarrass yourself and your team!

As a teenager, the most nerve-racking thing we can do is to take our driving test. Our parents risk their lives and others when they put us in the driver's seat. But they know we need to practice and prepare for the big test! Parallel parking, lane switching with a signal, even breaking at an intersection all take practice.

But without preparation, we will never succeed in driving and in life.

Here are some tips to help you with your preparation:

- **Do It the Night Before:** Preparing the night before can help you remedy any shortfalls that may occur. Do you ever find yourself scrambling to find clothes in the morning? Or looking for a missing item while rushing to get out the door? It would be so much easier if you'd simply set everything aside the night before.

- **When Possible, Do It Well in Advance:** The further in advance you prepare, the more time you have to remedy any unforeseen obstacles. Gather materials for that big event several days beforehand.

- **Do the Pre-work:** Preparation is about doing the work in advance. Read the materials. Review the data. Practice the activity. Be ready!

- **Save Time:** Some people will use the excuse that they don't have extra time to prepare in advance. Yet, preparing actually saves you time. It reduces errors, prevents re-work, and shortens activities.

- **Reduce Your Stress:** When you are ready, you are confident. When you are prepared, your stress is reduced because you have less to worry about.

- **Make It a Habit:** Make preparation part of your lifestyle, not something you do once in a blue moon. Preparation should be part of your daily habits.

I heard the following story from a trainer who worked with Kobe Bryant:

> I was invited to Las Vegas to help Team USA with their conditioning before they headed off to London for the Olympics. As we know, they eventually brought home the gold. I had the opportunity to work with Carmelo Anthony and Dwayne Wade in the past, but this would be my first interaction with Kobe Bryant.
> We first met three days before the first scrimmage. We had a brief conversation where we talked about conditioning. He took down

my number, and I let him know that if he ever wanted some extra training, he could call me any time.

The night before the first scrimmage, I was watching *Casablanca* for the first time. I was drifting off to sleep when my cell phone rang. It was Kobe.

I nervously answered.

Kobe said, "Hey, uh, Rob. I hope I'm not disturbing anything."

"No. What's up, Kobe?"

"Just wondering if you could help me out with some conditioning work."

I looked at the clock. 4:15 AM. "Yeah sure. I'll see you in the facility in a bit."

It took me about twenty minutes to get my gear and head out of the hotel. When I arrived and opened the door to the main practice floor, I saw Kobe. He was alone, drenched in sweat.

We did some conditioning work for the next hour and fifteen minutes. Then we entered the weight room, where he did a multitude of strength training exercises for the next 45 minutes. After that, we parted ways. I went back to the hotel and crashed, but he headed back to the practice floor.

I was expected to be at the floor again at 11:00 that morning. I woke up feeling drowsy. I silently and sarcastically thanked Kobe. Feeling sleep deprived, I grabbed a bagel and headed to the practice facility.

All the Team USA players were there, ready for the first scrimmage. LeBron was talking to

Carmelo, and Coach Krzyzewski was trying to explain something to Kevin Durant. On the right side of the practice facility was Kobe shooting jumpers by himself.

I went over and patted him on the back. "Good work this morning."

"Huh?"

"The conditioning?" I reminded him. "Good work."

"Oh yeah. Thanks Rob. I really appreciate it."

"So when did you finish?"

"Finish what?" Kobe asked.

"Getting your shots up. What time did you leave the facility?"

"Oh just now. I wanted 800 makes. So yeah, just now." He smiled.

My jaw dropped. Mother of holy God...

When you look at what Kobe Bryant accomplished over his amazing career, you would think he could take his foot off the gas occasionally. But no, not Kobe. That's why he is one of the greats.

Preparation gives you the best fighting chance. Like any well-built building, it all starts with a good foundation. If you skimp on your foundation, any success you have in life will be on shaky ground. But when you have a good foundation, you can keep growing and being more and more successful. So make sure you do your preparation in life.

PRINCIPLE 8

Raise Your Standards

The quality of a leader is reflected in the standards they set for themselves.

- Ray Kroc

As you pursue greatness, your standards must grow with you. There will come a certain point where most of the things that you used to do won't fit where you are in life. I'm not saying to forget what got you to this point in life, but you must accept growth and continue to raise the bar with everything you do.

When you raise the bar, the people who continue to stick around will be the ones who will help you go to the next level. The ones who fall away will become jealous of your rapid success.

Beware of those who do not share your visions, goals, and standards of living because they are likely to pull you back. Your growth makes them aware of what they have not achieved. It is easier for them to pull you down than to actually make changes in their own lives.

When I was developing into a star student athlete, I came to a number of crossroads. I had accepted that things were going to be different for me; therefore, my standards had to change. There were no late nights hanging out, smoking, or drinking for me. I had to learn how to maximize my time on the weekends. While others were partying it up, I was working planning the next game, completing school assignments, and preparing for up-coming interviews.

I was very fortunate to have some amazing people and mentors around me to help with the process. It was not easy working so hard in school and on the field, but I knew it was what needed to happen if I was going to reach the next level.

Every new opportunity allowed me to raise the bar for what I was doing and who I was becoming. You too have the power to grow and raise the bar! Why settle for being and doing average?

Set High, but Reachable, Goals

The goals you set for yourself have to be something you can reach! It would be ridiculous to say you want to snatch 700 pounds. No one on the planet can do that. Is there a more achievable goal? One that you can reach if you dedicate enough time and effort?

Here are four easy steps that will help you to raise your standards and create what you want:

1. **Believe**: The definition of the word *believe* is, "To accept as true or real, to have firm faith, confidence or trust." The first step in creating

Chronicle / Kurt Rogers

anything that you want is believing that it is possible to achieve it, and then having the knowingness that it will show up in your life. Anything is possible if you just believe and have the knowingness that it will manifest in your life

2. **Visualize**: What is it that you want? Think BIG. Getting clear and specific in your mind about what you want is absolutely necessary. Creating a vision board is a great way to visualize. You can also set aside a specific amount of time each day to visualize what it is that you want. This is literally like planning your future. The thoughts you have are critical in the manifestation process, so what will you continually "think" about?

3. **Feeling**: One of the key elements when you are visualizing what it is that you want is the feeling that accompanies it. Whenever we "want" something, it is usually the feeling that we want when we "have" that something. If we can feel the feeling of having whatever we want before it appears in its physical form, the manifestation process will occur more quickly. Being aware of your feelings is key when raising your standards.

4. **Action**: Taking action steps is the last part of raising our standards. When our believing, thinking, and feeling are all in alignment, the most important step is taking action on whatever it is that we want. But the action we are taking should not be manipulative nor controlling;

instead it must be in alignment with what we want. Taking action shows the Universe that we are not only ready to receive, but we are committed to what it is that we want.

Raise your standards, set your goals high, and go hunt them down.

PRINCIPLE 9

Change Your Limiting Beliefs!

We can either watch life from the sidelines, or actively participate... Either we let self-doubt and feelings of inadequacy prevent us from realizing our potential, or embrace the fact that when we turn our attention away from ourselves, our potential is limitless.
                                    - Christopher Reeve

Your mindset is everything. Fortunately, my mother and family helped me understand that I could do anything I wanted in life. It was only a matter of following though.

The problem is most people focus on failure. When they begin to think about what they want in life, they focus on what bad might happen. They limit their potential when they create negative beliefs. The bad that they focus on will likely never happen, but their negativity still stops them from even trying!

Where do limiting beliefs come from? When we are born, we have a clear mind. Over the years, we start to hear and see things that develop "I can't" thoughts. Unfortunately, these messages come from the most influential people around us, like our parents and teachers.

As we start to believe what we are told, limiting beliefs put us in an imaginary box. We start to believe things like, "I'm too short," "My parents couldn't achieve it either," "I don't have the resources," "I don't have the finances," and so on.

If a friend kept telling you that a crate is very heavy, that it weighs over 200 pounds, you might not try to lift it! In such a case, you acquired the limiting belief from your friend. On their statement alone, you decided you couldn't lift the crate, even though you never tested the crate nor your ability to lift it. Maybe your friend was wrong. Or maybe you are strong enough to lift it.

You Are More Than You Think You Are

1. What is your most debilitating limiting belief?

2. Why do you have this limiting belief?

3. What would you do with your life if you no longer had this limiting belief?

4. What do you think the odds are of the worst thing happening?

5. What are three to five small, manageable actions you could take on your goal this week while your limiting belief is sealed in an envelope?

The media, our friends, our relatives, and the people we come in contact with feed us limiting beliefs without our notice. People live without self confidence just because they absorbed the limiting beliefs imposed on them by others!

Limiting beliefs can prevent you from reaching your potential, succeeding in life, and they can make you miserable. One of the biggest differences between those who succeed and those who don't is the ability to locate and eliminate limiting beliefs.

You can eliminate many limiting beliefs and manage others so they aren't as powerful or debilitating. As you cut the legs out from under these beliefs, they will begin to loosen their hold over you. Once you do this, you can reclaim the enthusiasm and energy you need to recreate your life.

- You will do things you never thought possible
- You will take actions that make things happen
- You will find passion in life and seize every opportunity
- You will have the ability to push through fear to achieve big things

PRINCIPLE 10
Create a Culture

A nation's culture resides in the hearts and in the soul of its people.

- Mahatma Gandhi

Positive energy is everything! And having great people to be around is key! You want to create a culture that is supported by the people in your life.

When I say to create a culture, this is your opportunity to live your life and go about your daily endeavors as you please. Of course, we all have to follow rules and laws, but our ultimate goal is to create a great environment that contains like minded people with goals, dreams, great energy, and up lifting spirits.

There are plenty of ways that you can start creating the next level of life. There are a number avenues that you can seek to create a culture. They contain attributes for innovation, change, achievement, wellness, learning, and execution.

What do you see that is lacking in your community? What are your strong beliefs? Where do you see yourself improving and being a true leader?

As I strive to be the best businessman I can be, my goal is to create a culture for young entrepreneurs to have access to all of the business leads they could possibly have. What I have done with my current business venture, Rise Above Enterprise, is create an environment for networking with relentless winners who will come together and develop future business projects. These leaders come from across the world and are in every type of business.

By no means am I an expert in tech, chemistry, or other fields, but I know great people who are. I have developed a great skill for putting the correct people in the same room to develop grand projects. The culture that I have aimed to create takes a very experienced individual or company and connects them with entrepreneurs who possess true skills to create and the possibility to learn the tricks of the trade to develop their dreams. We want to create leaders! We seek individuals who have great business ideas and the

hunger to go through the process to develop into a true leader.

We can all relate to moments when we felt stuck trying to tap into our own creativity. This process is your mind at work. Your mind is creating all sorts of assumptions, self-imposed constraints, and limiting beliefs. We can remove these assumptions just by getting started. So, start doing and stop thinking.

Set Expectations

It is important to set firm, clear, and concise expectations for cultures you create. Accountability will not grow where team members are unsure of the group's purpose and vision. Cultures need to define what is expected of members before holding people accountable.

You can set expectations by:

- Clearly communicating the team's mission and vision.

- Emphasizing the urgency and importance of whatever task you have assigned.

- Laying out the standards that will be upheld throughout the process. Be specific regarding end results, time frames, and expected levels of effort.

- Clearly and explicitly define each member's role and responsibilities.

The clearer initial goals and expectations are, the less time will be spent arguing when someone is held accountable.

Invite Commitment

Although you may make these initial conditions and goals clear, it is important to have the team members commit to standards and expectations. Work with your team to make sure everyone commits to their role and understands how it will benefit both the individual and the team. Be sure to put it in writing, too. This will give the commitment a physical representation that cannot be debated.

Accountability grows when this connection is made, and it is enhanced when other people are aware of the commitment. Team members are further motivated to accomplish their tasks and will more readily welcome you holding them accountable for their actions or lack thereof.

Be a Model

The best way to create a stand-up organization is to lead by example. Make sure others understand what you expect of them, and that you're holding yourself to the same high standard. Follow through on your promises, own up to your mistakes, and give feedback even when it is not easy.

Coordinate Plans of Action

In order for plans of action to be successful, everyone must be on the same page. Coordination of activities increases efficiency and ensures successful execution of any plan. Coordinating plans of action leads to an improved collective focus on company goals and the successful execution of plans.

Create a Structure for Unstructured Time

Ideas need time to develop. No one ever feels like they have time to spare. People get so consumed with chasing short-term targets that they can't think about the future. But your creative mind needs time. So set aside time in your schedule for unstructured time when you can let your mind explore possibilities.

Persistence

Innovation involves more than just great ideas. We need faith, hard work, and a laser sharp focus on the end results. We tend to see the end result of a creative idea in awe, but what we don't see are the actions, hard work, and persistence that goes on behind the scenes to make the vision a reality. Without persistence, we'll give up when we face roadblocks. And there will always be roadblocks between you and your goals.

Remove Inhibitions

Under the spell of inhibition, we feel limited and stuck. We need to free ourselves from these mind-created constraints by removing assumptions and restrictions. This is what we refer to when we say, "think outside the box." Encourage yourself to be open to new ideas and solutions without setting limiting beliefs. Remember, innovation is more about psychology than intellect.

Take Risks, Make Mistakes

I believe that part of the reason why we create self-imposed inhibition is due to our fear of failure. Expect that some ideas will fail in the process of learning. Build prototypes, test them out on people, gather feedback, and make incremental changes. Rather than treating mistakes as failures, think of them as experiments you make on your way to launching your true purpose.

Scott Berkun said, "Experiment is the expected failure to deliberately learn something." Instead of punishing yourself for failures, accept them, then take your newfound knowledge and put it toward finding the best solution. Live up to your goal of producing the best result, but understand you might make mistakes along the way. And make sure you learn from mistakes.

Escape

Our environment can and does affect how we feel. The more relaxed and calm we are internally, the more receptive we are to creativity. This is why ideas sometimes come to us in the shower or while we're alone.

Each of us has different triggers to access our creative energy. For instance, I get into the 'creative zone' from sitting at my dining table, with a warm cup of chai, and my noise-canceling headphones. Many great thinkers go on long walks to help them solve problems. Experiment and find what works for you.

Writing Things Down

Many innovators and creative people keep a journal to jot down ideas and thoughts as they occur. Some of them keep a sketch book, scrap book, post-it notes, or loose paper nearby. They all have a method to capture their thoughts, to think on paper, to drop their inhibitions and to start the creative process. Just to show how important this creative process is, Leonardo Da Vinci's famous notebook was purchased by Bill Gates for $30.8 million dollars.

Factors for Creating a Culture of Change

Inspire: Develop leadership that sets a clear vision for the future, which is both closely tied to goals and the new emphasis that comes from change. The key to inspiration, which many people forget, is that it must be sustained and evolve over time.

Support: Support takes many forms, from a new lead for your business, to experiential training, to access to assets, or a competition for the budget. The common factor is that support makes the vision tangible and invites others to engage with the vision.

Manifest: Both vision and tangible expressions provide a story and a way to make the story real. For an organization to experience success, the new way of thinking must fully come to life. Usually, change is first manifested through pilot programs initiated to demonstrate profit or success, which are then expanded and further adopted through new processes.

Once we have a culture of change, we will have success. We will notice opportunities and be ready to exploit them. Best of all, our team will be there to support us.

PRINCIPLE 11

Let Go of the Past

Do not dwell in the past, do not dream of the future, concentrate the mind on the present moment.

- Buddha

The one-hour flight from San Fransisco to Eugene, Oregon, felt like ten hours. As we began our approach to Eugene, I looked out the airplane window. I saw clouds covering the trees with mountains in the distance. What should have been the most exciting day of my life was actually the heaviest-hearted day because the seat next to me was empty.

Stepping off the plane in Eugene, I was amazed by the crisp, clean air. It wasn't anything like my home town.

I was away from home for the first time, ready to become a man and enjoy all the experiences life had for me. At the same time, the pain in my heart seemed to never stop.

As the shuttle drove us to the campus, I saw the giant Oregon Ducks "O" sitting effortlessly atop of the beautiful Autzen Stadium. This is where our dreams were supposed to come true. This is where we were supposed to go into battle together. In football practice, we would bring the best out of one another. This is where we would hold hands and run out of the tunnel on game day, just like we did as De La Salle Spartans.

As I entered the locker room, I was greeted with blank stares from teammates who I had not yet gotten the chance to know. But they knew me. They knew that I had arrived on campus empty, damaged, and grieving even though I had a smile on my face for the cameras.

You see, my brother, Terrance Kelly (TK), did not get on that airplane with me. He had been gunned down a few days earlier.

On the day that TK was taken from us, we chatted on the phone. We where supposed to get together and workout, but TK said, "Hey Bro, not going to make the workout."

I said "What do you mean? I'm here waiting on you."

TK said, "I have to run some errands and handle some things before we leave. I was going to whoop you in the drills anyway."

"You wish! Okay, you owe me one." It was the last thing I said to TK.

Later that night, as I was having dinner, my godfather came downstairs with a look on his face like he had seen a ghost.

"What's wrong?" I asked.

He said with a monotone, "TK was shot and killed."

This could not be real. First my parents, and now my best friend? I ran to my bedroom to check my cell phone. Forty-three missed calls! Family, teammates, friends.

The first call I made was to TJ Ward. He answered the phone, distraught. He had heard, but was not sure what exactly happened.

My next call was to Jackie Bates. He was at the scene by the time I got him on the phone. He confirmed that it was true, "There is blood everywhere."

I couldn't imagine what he was seeing. I ran back to my godfather, who was now on the phone with someone who was with the family. I heard screaming and yelling over the phone, "TK! TK! No! Not TK." It was a nightmare.

My brother was gunned down in a senseless act of violence. And my life has forever been changed.

I share this event because letting go of the past is very import for moving forward in the right way with the right energy! I've had every opportunity to quit and walk away from it all. I could have been angry at the world, shut myself off, not cared about anything. But I fought through the pain, and came to a point to where I realized that life will give us trials and hurdles. It is on us to figure out our path. As much as it hurts to not have my parents or TK physically here, I have dedicated my life to them, using that hurt as motivation to positively and creatively reach new heights!

Wherever you are reading this, there is something from your past that is affecting your performance or creating negative energy. It may be potentially blocking you from your calling!

You control your destiny. You control your emotions. Let your past go! Free your heart, mind, and spirit. Move forward toward your dreams!

Tips for Letting Go of the Past and Embracing the Future

Focus: Find peace. Breathe. Focus is an action. Our minds are much harder to quiet than our bodies. Our lives are busy and fast paced, filled with external noise and distractions. Clarity comes from quiet. Meditation, even in small amounts, will make room for the next nine tips.

Understand: Take time to reflect on your own history as a third party. Look in without judgment. Simply observe. Understand that you are not your past. Understand that the situations and patterns and people in your life created your experiences; they didn't create you. Knowing and understanding your past and some of your patterns will help you to recognize why you hold on to and repeat self-destructive behaviors. Understanding creates awareness, and awareness helps you break the cycle.

Accept: Accept your history and the people who have been a part of your life. Accept your circumstances and remember that none of these things define you. Acceptance is an important step to letting go and setting yourself free.

Empty your cup: Consciously and actively work at letting go of your story. It has no real value. They do not make you stronger, healthier, or more powerful. Pour out your expectations of how, who, where, and what you should be. These beliefs are part of a story that holds you back from simply being. Once you let go of this story, and empty your cup, your life purpose will open up and flow.

Align: Take a moment (or several—you're worth the time) to write down the following:

1. Your core beliefs and values
2. Your life goals
3. The actions that you are taking to pursue those goals

Now take an honest look at your core beliefs and values to determine whether or not they align with your goals and actions. If not, ask yourself if it is time to create new core beliefs, set new goals, or take new actions? Write down three actions that you will take this week to get yourself moving.

Flex: It may seem paradoxical to detach from outcomes, while setting goals and working toward them. But if you are flexible—that is, willing to let go of the end result—aligning your goals and true purpose with the greater good is righteous action. Be flexible; allow the path to unfold as it will, opening up to opportunities. Flex and flow with the current of life.

Contribute: When you find yourself lamenting about your past, or angry about your present, or brooding about your future, find a way to make someone else's day better. Offering a smile to someone as you pass, opening a door, putting a bit of extra change in the parking meter, dropping off some food for the food bank, these simple actions can have lasting impact and help you to put your situation into perspective. Contributing to the well-being of others is the best way to align with your true self.

Believe in yourself: Believe in your purpose. Believe that the universe is unfolding as it should, and that you have a divine role to play. Believe that holding on does nothing but hold you back from that purpose.

Love the process: Have fun. Be playful, cheerful, and positive. Give power to positivity. Love yourself, love others, and love this life. It is a gift to unwrap each and every day, to gaze upon it with new and excited eyes.

Be grateful: Be true. Once you have taken all of these actions, say "thank you" to the Universe.

Once you let go of the past and embrace the future, you will truly live up to your purpose.

PRINCIPLE 12

Don't Give Up

"The world's greatest achievers have been those who have always stayed focused on their goals and have been consistent in their efforts."
- Dr Roopleen

In life, we will face plenty of adversity that will potentially cause us to want to give up. Events will not always go our way, bad things happen, or we may not receive the outcome we planned for. What do we do then?

We have two choices: we can either take what has happened and improve the situation ourselves, or we can go the easy route and give up. If we give up, we will never experience what we wanted in life.

My father passed when I was six. It was my time to step up and learn how to be the man of the house. But when my mother slipped into a coma and passed away weeks before my sixteenth birthday, the weight of the world was on my shoulders. It was a crushing blow, almost too much to bear.

5 Reasons To Not Give Up

1. There is a purpose for each of us waiting to be found

2. What gives life meaning is the struggle that we live through

3. A helping hand can always be found if needed

4. Success feels great

5. Inspire others

My sister and I knew that we had serious choices to make. We could strive to continue the legacy our parents had instilled with us, or we could give up and go on to lead unproductive lives. I chose to continue my focus on school and becoming the best football player I could possibly be. That was my motivation! My parents' deaths became my "tragedy into triumph." My goal was to not give up. As much as it hurt to not have them here, I had to make them proud and carry on our family name!

Game Day

As a senior at the University of Oregon, I kicked everything into gear; I was playing my best football ever! I was pro-ready, big, strong, fast, smart, and playing for the hottest offense in the NCAA. Leading the Pac 10 at the time in receiving, I knew that this was my year to solidify my name in the NFL draft.

Then a missed block and a twist of my ankle left me crumpling to the turf. You could hear a pin drop in the Autzen Stadium filled with 70,000 fans. Teammates, coaches, and staff surrounded me. The looks on their faces said it all, "Is this it?"

This was the time to give up on my dream and walk away. But not me! As I waited in the locker room for doctors to tell me my fate, I said, "I will wear a jersey again."

When the doctors came in, they let me know that I had shattered my right ankle, torn extensive ligaments that would need surgery, and I would be sidelined for 8 to 12 months for recovery and rehab. What they didn't know was that the NFL combine was three months away, and the NFL draft was five months away!

As I wiped the tears, I said to myself, "I have faced some for the darkest moments attending the funerals of some of the dearest people to me. This ankle injury will be easy to overcome."

Dreams Come True

One titanium plate and eight screws were inserted into my right ankle. I had to wear a cast for nearly eight weeks.

Once that cast came off, it was time to go to work. Along with going to school to complete my classes for my degree, my schedule was jam packed with rehab. As I progressed, my mindset was clear. I knew that I would not be fully ready to perform for the NFL scouts in April, but I also knew that I would show the scouts that I was a talented player, who was hardworking and disciplined, and who was willing to display my love for the game through my relentless work ethic.

I flew to Orlando, Florida, to rehab with a specialist who was a gold medalist and once the world's fastest man, Dennis Mitchell. When I arrived, I could not even stand on my feet and walk, let alone run. The work began with grueling two or three workouts a day. Late nights, I would complete course work for school, rest, and get right back at it the next day. Most weeks, I would fly back to Eugene to attend class.

Time flew by, and before I knew it, I was standing in front of 32 teams getting ready to perform. I had received numerous interests from NFL teams. In the weeks leading up to the draft, I attended private workouts from the interested teams. I gave it my best.

I continued to rehab and work out in the weeks leading up to the draft. I had every expectation that a team would pick me up.

When the big day came, of course I was anxious. Who would call? How long would I have to wait?

Then my phone rang. It was the general manager from the San Francisco 49ers. "Cameron, are you ready to be a 49er?"

What if I had given up when times were difficult? What if I had given up on my dreams when my father

passed? Or if grief had caused me to stop after my mother died? What if I hadn't given it my all in Oregon after TK was shot and killed? Or what if I'd let my ankle injury keep me from trying for the draft? Believe me, there were many other opportunities and temptations to give up or put things off along the way.

If I had let just one of the those events slow me down or get me down, I would have never experienced what it is like to be a professional football player, much less a member of such an iconic team as the San Francisco 49ers.

Everything I've shared with you in this book has been for one purpose—to inspire you, to give you a path to build toward your own success and your own dreams.

When I tell you stories from my own life, I want them to be examples for you. It is my hope that when you are faced with difficulties, that you will realize that someone has gone through something similar, maybe something worse, and he went on to realize his dreams.

I don't know what your dreams are, but I do know that you will not only accomplish them, but also experience the incredible excitement that comes from achievement. Along the way, though, you must never give up, because if you do, you'll never know what it is like to achieve your full potential.

Believe me, there is nothing better than setting a high goal for yourself, and then achieving it! Now is your time! Let's get started, and never give up!

Conclusion

The Ultimate Focus

The road to success requires sacrifice, and it takes patience. You will have to keep your focus five or ten years down the road. That is when you will reap the rewards from your efforts today. The process of getting there is full of challenges and pleasures. Nothing worthwhile comes easily. You can ask any successful person about their journey, and they will tell you a great story of challenges and victories.

Remember that people are not aware of their ultimate interests or future career paths as a child. Over the years, we learn more about ourselves and our talents. And we become painfully aware of own limitations. But it is up to each of us to create our own stories of achievement. It is up to us to first learn what we truly want in life, and then strive to overcome our limitations and the obstacles life puts in our path.

Many people look at obstacles and their own limitations and give up. They became afraid. They make excuses as to why they did not achieve their dreams. These individuals never receive the great feeling of success. Worse, they discourage others.

It is important to remember that you are not a product of your environment; you are merely a product of your mind state and inner drive. This places all the responsibility on you!

Nothing good can ever come from deviating from the path you were destined to follow. It is up to you and only you to understand and see the signs in life and to continue to push on.

Most people will be side-tracked by money or immediate pleasure. When you take the easy route, you are moving yourself further and further away from your path. Very soon, you will end up on multiple dead ends. Importantly, even if your material needs are met, you will feel an emptiness inside that you will need to fill.

I can personally tell you that, in the end, the money and success that will truly last, will only come to those who focus on fulfilling their life's purpose.

What are you called to do? Where do you see yourself doing the most good? How will you be able to truly give back?

Wherever life takes you, and whatever your dreams may be, promise yourself that you will Neverstop.